# THE *FANTASTIC* BOOK OF
# *Mountain*
# BIKING

## BRANT RICHARDS

## COPPER BEECH BOOKS
## BROOKFIELD, CONNECTICUT

© Aladdin Books Ltd 1998

*Designed and
produced by*
Aladdin Books Ltd
28 Percy Street
London W1P 0LD

*First published in the United States
in 1998 by*
Copper Beech Books,
an imprint of
The Millbrook Press
2 Old New Milford Road
Brookfield, Connecticut 06804

*Editor*
Sarah Levete
*Design*
David West Children's
Book Design
*Designer*
Flick Killerby
*Illustrators*
Catherine Ward (Simon Girling &
Associates) and Rob Shone
*Picture Research*
Brooks Krikler Research

Printed in Belgium

Library of Congress
Cataloging-in-Publication Data
Richards, Brant.
Mountain biking / Brant Richards ;
illustrated by Catherine Ward and Rob Shone.
p. cm. — (The fantastic book of—)
Includes index.
Summary: Provides step-by-step instructions
for both basic techniques and more advanced
tricks to be used in mountain biking.
ISBN 0-7613-0725-7 (trade : hc). —
ISBN 0-7613-0718-4 (lib.bdg.)
1. All terrain cycling—Juvenile literature.
[1. All terrain cycling.]  I. Ward, Catherine, ill.
II. Shone, Rob, ill.  III. Title.  IV. Series.
GV1056.R537 1998            97-35114
796.6'3—dc21                CIP  AC
5 4 3 2 1

# CONTENTS

# Introduction

Millions of people, of all ages, enjoy the thrill and freedom of riding on a mountain bike. A mountain bike makes it easy to speed up, and down, even the steepest hills and to ride over the bumpiest terrain. From riding along a muddy trail with friends to downhill racing, riding a mountain bike offers it all — fresh air, fitness, and fun.

To begin mountain biking, all you need to do is buy or rent a mountain bike and a helmet from one of the many specialty stores, where sales assistants can help you to select the right equipment. Find a stretch of flat ground away from traffic — and read on.

Whether or not you are an experienced rider, this book tells you everything you need to know, from care of your bike to bunny-hopping over logs on the trail.

An eight-page fold-out shows you what happens at major mountain bike events and competitions, from cross-country racing to trials riding. It shows you how the professionals cope with the demands of a challenging four-hour ride or performing incredible stunts in incredible places!

Mountain biking is a lot of fun — but it can also be demanding and dangerous. Whether you ride on quiet country roads or go "off-road" in the hills, always put safety first. This involves understanding how your bike works (*see pages 12-13*), knowing how to check it properly before every ride (*see pages 30-31*), being aware of other road or countryside users, and only attempting moves that you can perform safely.

With your sense of safety and fun, put on your helmet, get on your mountain bike, and get pedaling!

## ON YOUR BIKE!

You can ride a mountain bike on city streets, or you can go "off-road," riding in the open countryside.

When you have practiced the basic riding techniques (*see pages 14-15*), and you feel safe and confident on your bike, try out some of the different types of mountain bike riding, from riding trails (routes through the countryside, *below*) to tricks (*see pages 34-35*).

## COMPETITION TIME

As a mountain biker you can simply hit the trail with a friend and just enjoy the ride, or you can take the sport more seriously (*above*) by entering different competitive events. From cross-country racing (*see page 18*) to downhill racing (*see pages 19-22*), there are events for everyone. Check out mountain biking magazines or specialized stores for up-to-date information on events that you can enter.

*Whatever your level of riding and whatever the type of riding you are involved in, stay safe. Only attempt moves or ride distances for which you have the necessary skills and strength.*

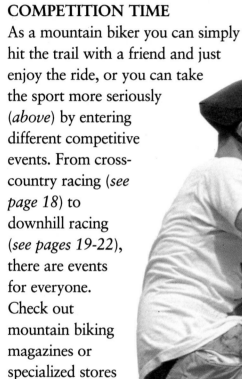

### TIME FOR TRICKERY

*Many riders enjoy the thrill of stunt riding. This involves tricks such as the "wheelie" (right). Wait until you are an experienced and skilled rider before you attempt a stunt.*

# Taking up
# MOUNTAIN BIKING

Mountain biking is one of the most exciting sports you can enjoy. A mountain bike is often easier to ride than a regular road bike — its chunky tires, wide range of gears, and powerful brakes make it easy to cross even the roughest terrain. A mountain bike reaches the places that other bikes cannot reach, from woody tracks to steep hills.

**ON THE TRAIL**
*When you are on a trail ride, make sure that you carry tools and spares for your bike.*

**REASONS TO RIDE**
"You can just put on your helmet, get on your bike, and be out in the fresh air in no time. It's a great sport for girls and boys... It's excellent to go out on a ride with your friends... There are so many tricks to learn... It doesn't matter if you're a beginner — you can always have a good time."

# Anatomy of a MOUNTAIN BIKE

A mountain bike, like any other bike, consists of a frame to which wheels and other components, such as brakes, gears, and pedals, are attached.

The parts that make a mountain bike look different from other bikes are its large tires, its set of three chainrings, which gives it low gears for hill climbing (*see pages 14-15*), and its flat handlebars, fitted with powerful brake levers.

**MOUNTAIN BIKE BRAKES**
To make the brakes on a mountain bike powerful enough to stop the bike quickly and to allow the bike to be ridden through mud without jamming up, the brakes are fitted to a specially welded part of the frame.

Seat

Seat post

Seat tube

Rear brake

Seat stays

The **front derailleur** *moves the chain across the chainrings.*

Rim

Sprockets

Chainrings

Chain stays

Crank

The **rear derailleur** *moves the chain from gear to gear across the chainrings and sprockets (see pages 14-15), derailing it.*

## GETTING IN GEAR

The mountain bike pictured has gear shifters, operated by the rider turning the handlebar grips. Other mountain bikes may have push button gear shifters or simple gear levers.

Handlebar

Gear shifter

Brake lever

Stem

Headset

Top tube

Head tube

Headset

Front brake cable

Fork

Down tube

Spoke

Tire

Pedal

The **hub** contains the axle and bearings to keep the wheel in place.

# Buying your MOUNTAIN BIKE

The best place to buy a mountain bike is from a specialized mountain bike store. The staff will be able to advise you on which bike is the best for you — from the size of the frame to the type of tires for the sort of riding you're going to do. They will make sure that your bike is safe to ride — you won't have to put it together yourself!

More expensive bikes are lighter and stronger, but don't think you have to spend hundreds of dollars to enjoy yourself on a bike. Whichever mountain bike you choose, you'll enjoy the ride as long as the bike is safe and right for you.

### WHICH ONE?

*There are literally hundreds of different bikes* (above) *to choose from. Ask the store assistant to help you make the best choice.*

1

2

3

### WHAT DO YOU GET FOR YOUR MONEY?

*The best mountain bikes can cost over $6,000, but don't worry — you can buy one for much less! The type of metal used in the frame* (see opposite page), *and the bike's suspension, if any, will affect the bike's price. The suspension consists of springs and pistons that absorb bumps in the ground when you ride over them. A basic, cheap mountain bike has a rigid frame, with no suspension* 1 *. A bike with front suspension* 2 *costs more, but not as much as the ultimate in comfort — a bike with front and rear suspension* 3 *.*

### SIZE IS EVERYTHING!

When you choose a mountain bike to buy or to rent, it is very important that it is the right size for you.

Stand with the bike between your legs and your feet flat on the floor. Make sure that there are at least 2 inches (5 cm) between the top of your legs and the top tube of the bike, as you straddle the bike, standing near the seat.

If the distance is any less than this, it could hurt if you crash!

Ask a sales assistant in a mountain bike store to help make sure that the bike is suitable for your size (*left*).

## IT'S ALL IN A FRAME

Mountain bike frames come in a range of different metals. These vary in strength and weight. The top-range, and most expensive, frame will be made of a very light but strong material, such as titanium (*below left*). A frame made from an aluminum alloy — aluminum mixed with other metals (*below right*) — is heavier than titanium but will be less expensive. A standard, cheap mountain bike frame is usually made from steel (*top right*). This is hard-wearing, but it can be very heavy.

*DON'T WAIT!*
*Make sure your bike is right for you now, rather than waiting to grow into it. If you look after your bike well, you can sell it once you have outgrown it — then you will be able to buy another bike that fits you.*

11

Put your **helmet** on, whenever you are on your bike.

A **waterproof jacket** over a T-shirt and sweatshirt will help keep you warm.

Wear **cycling gloves** with fingers to keep your hands warm and dry in the winter months.

**Waterproof pants** over sweatpants or cycling shorts will keep you dry.

You will need a pair of strong **sneakers** or **mountain bike shoes**.

## WHAT TO WEAR

Every time you ride your bike make sure you wear a helmet and that it is fastened and adjusted correctly. Wearing gloves can keep you from hurting your hands if you fall. It can also keep the handlebar grips from rubbing against your hands and making them sore. Wear either special mountain-biking shoes or hard-wearing sneakers. Remember, the correct clothes will give you a more comfortable ride!

# Safety and COMFORT

Mountain biking is great fun... but it can also be dangerous. Always wear the appropriate protective clothing and equipment, from gloves to a helmet. A helmet is a vital piece of equipment. Mountain biking can be a year-round sport but you need different clothes for different times of the year to keep cool in warmer months (*far right*) and warm and dry in colder months (*left*).

### WHY WEAR A HELMET?
If you fall off a mountain bike and hit your head hard on the ground while not wearing a helmet, you could die. Always wear a helmet. It will protect your head from injury if you crash or get knocked off your bike. When a helmet absorbs the impact of a crash it, may crack or collapse. You cannot always see a crack so you must replace your helmet after it has been knocked.

## SEAT HEIGHT

Get your seat at the right height — it will give you more pedal power. Ask a friend to help set the seat height so that one of your legs is nearly straight when one of the pedals is at its lowest point (*left*).

If the seat is too low, you may be able to reach the ground more easily, but riding will be harder work. Riding with a low seat can also damage your knees.

*A **helmet** for any weather.*

*Wear a **cycling T-shirt**, made from material to keep your body cool in the heat and warm in colder temperatures.*

***BE CAREFUL***
*Crashes can, and do, occur when you're mountain biking. But you can help prevent serious injury if you take the trouble to learn how to fall (see below) and wear the correct equipment and clothing (right).*

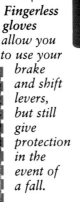

*Fingerless gloves allow you to use your brake and shift levers, but still give protection in the event of a fall.*

*Cycling shorts have a padded lining. Wear them without underwear to prevent chafing from the seat.*

## CRASHING SAFELY

Just in case you do crash or fall, it's important to know how to fall safely. If you realize you are about to crash, try to get the bike onto its side, skidding the tires by braking to reduce the speed as much as possible. If you can, jump clear of the bike. Avoid sticking an arm out straight because this can easily lead to a painful break of your collarbone.

TAKING CORNERS
To ride a bike in a circle, don't just turn the handlebars. Lean slightly toward the direction that you want to go.
The faster you go, the more you need to lean.

# Learning TO RIDE

When you have set the seat at the correct height (*see page 13*), and you have made your pre-ride checks (*see page 31*), you can start pedaling. Find a flat area away from moving or parked cars, where you can practice operating the gears and brakes. Practice riding in circles, stopping quickly, and accelerating away from a standstill using your gears to help give you more speed.

When you are used to the way your bike works, or "handles," you can ride in the real world.

## SHIFTING GEARS

The range of mountain bike gears (which can be up to 24) allow you to pedal at the same rate, however steep the terrain, or ground, over which you are riding. The number of gears on your bike depends on how many chainrings and sprockets (*see pages 8–9*) there are on the bike.

Chainrings are the cogs attached to the cranks, and sprockets are the cogs on the rear wheel. There are usually three chainrings and seven or eight sprockets.

A click or shift of your left-hand gear lever, or shifter, moves the chainrings; the right-hand gear lever, or shifter, moves the sprockets. From any one of the three chainrings (low, middle, and high, *see below*), you can fine-tune the gear you are in by shifting the sprockets with the right-hand gear lever.

## PUT YOUR BRAKES ON!
Your mountain bike has a very powerful front and rear brake fitted to the frame (*below*). The brakes are operated by the brake levers on the handlebars. The right-hand lever operates the rear brake, and the left-hand lever operates the front brake. Be careful when you use the front brake — if you pull too hard on it the bike may tip forward, taking you with it! If you pull too hard on the rear brake the back wheel will skid. Try to balance the braking power between your front and rear brakes.

PEDALING
Keep the ball of your foot over the center of the pedal to make pedaling easier. This will also help you to keep better control of the bike.

## *RULES ON THE ROAD*
When you are riding on a road, ride about a foot from the edge of the sidewalk, keeping clear of drains and gutters. Look ahead and be careful, especially at intersections when cars could either be pulling out or turning across your path. The road is no place to practice tricks or stunts — save those for safe areas away from cars. Turn to pages 16 and 38 for further rules for riding off-road.

The high chainring on the bottom three sprockets ①  is for downhill riding. The low chainring on the top three sprockets ②  is for climbing hills. The middle chainring on the top three sprockets ③  is for riding on the flat.

**3**

**2**

**1**

* Unless you are racing or riding up a steep hill, ride in the middle chainring.

*GEAR TIPS*
* Avoid changing gear when you are pedaling hard.

15

*Even when you ride in the countryside you will meet traffic, such as walkers and horse riders (above). Learn the rules of the road — this will help to keep you safe for town riding and off-road riding.*

# Where to GO RIDING

On your mountain bike, you can ride on any roads where cars are allowed. In the countryside, you can also ride on public trails. You are not allowed to ride on sidewalks — these are for walkers only. If you stay on public trails and always yield to walkers you'll stay safe and you won't get into any trouble.

*Wherever you ride your bike (above), be courteous and polite to other trail users.*

## HELP, I'M LOST!

To avoid getting lost:

❋ Ride with a responsible older rider (*right*) who knows the route.

❋ Tell your parent or caregiver where you are going and at what time you will return.

❋ Never ride by yourself — you could fall and no one would be able to get you help.

If you do get lost, try to retrace your route until you come to a landmark that you recognize.

# Competition Events

## WHO, WHEN, AND WHERE?

During the summer, mountain bike events are held every weekend throughout the country. The main competitive events are downhill and dual slalom (*see pages 19-22*), cross-country (*left and see page 18*), and trials riding (*see page 24*).

### GETTING INVOLVED

*Although most professional riders specialize in one type of competition event, you can try them all. Pick up details of events and entry forms from a bike store or a mountain biking magazine. Riders of all levels can enter a race or competitive event. Most competition categories include beginner for the first-time competitor; sport for the intermediate rider; and expert for the advanced rider. The pro or elite category is for the professional rider.*

## AGAINST THE ELEMENTS

Although a mass of riders may start together (*above*), soon the stronger riders will break away from the crowd to take the lead. In mountain bike events, the rider is competing against other riders as well as facing the challenges of the terrain (*left*)!

*Getting wet*

## DUAL SLALOM

Dual slalom racing (*right*) is a competition event in which two riders race each other down a course marked by slalom poles. The course is made up of two lanes of equal length, usually marked in red and blue. Dual slalom is an exciting event to watch as competitors speed down the track, trying to avoid each other, but often crashing.

*Downhill bike tires (above) are bigger than those on a standard bike. They have a tough "tread" pattern to help prevent flat tires.*

# Going Downhill!

## DOWNHILL RACING

Downhill and dual slalom are the most exciting sports in mountain biking to take part in and to watch (*right*). Racing against the clock, downhill riders complete the marked course as quickly as possible. Downhill cours are made up of natural and artificial obstacles. Cour designers use earth-moving equipment to create jum and "bermed" corners for riders to negotiate at high speeds. Downhill riders can reach speeds of over 60 mph (96 km/h).

*3 - 2 - 1 - GO!*
*The racer must accelerate as fast as possible onto the course* (above) *to guarantee a good time at the finish.*

## HARD AND FAST

A downhill racer has to have the power and fitness to pedal hard and fast throughout the course (*right*), even when the course obstacles force the rider to reduce his or her speed.

# Cross-Country

## A TOUGH COURSE

In a cross-country race, competitors speed around a marked course for a specific number of laps. The winner is the rider to finish first — simple. Except it's not quite so simple — at a top-level event, competitors may be riding for up to four hours, battling against rough ground and obstacles.

*It's great fun watching a downhill race event.*

*The cheers of the crowds encourage the riders.*

### THE COURSE

*A lap of a good cross-country course will feature most hazards that you're likely to find on a real bike ride. Climbs (above), descents, trees, mud, rocks, and all sorts of other natural hazards are sure to be on the course.*

*It's usually on the uphill climb that a competitor can gain extra time in the cross-country race.*

*Cross-country races have different classes for riders to enter, depending on their age or ability. Whatever a rider's level, he or she may well come face to face with nature (right)!*

# Trials

In a trials event the rider wants as few points as possible. Mistakes mean points and the rider with the fewest points wins! Trials riders aim to complete a marked course full of obstacles, such as huge logs (*right*), without putting a foot down on the ground, a move that is known as a dab.

a dual
...om, it's just
two of you!

### RIDING ON THE EDGE
*These riders seem to be riding up a hill — but they are actually riding on top of a sloping wall!*

...als are fun
...watch —
...risky to
...form.

Many riders begin their competitive mountain biking careers at an early age.

*These stunts should only be performed by the most experienced trail riders who combine exceptional balance skills with great bravery.*

### WHAT NEXT?
Trials are not timed and competitors can ride the different course obstacles in any order they wish. Watched by judges, trials riders have to cope with the most ingenious and extraordinary obstacles (*right*). No two trials courses are the same.

**SOMEBODY'S WATCHING**
As crowds are cheering the riders (*far left*), judges will be watching and monitoring them throughout the race (*left*). Judges and officials time the riders and check that all the rules are observed — confirming at the end of the race that there was no foul play!

*ynhill bike (above and bottom left)
bike used on trails. It has a full
1 (see pages 34-35), similar to a
1 on a motorcycle. Powerful disk
der to stop the bike quickly.*

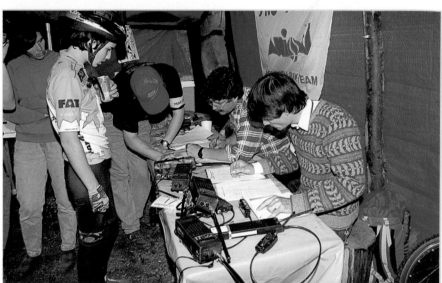

*CRASH, BANG,... SAFE!*
*Crashes are part of the course in a downhill race or a dual slalom event. To save themselves from injury, all riders wear protective body armor, similar to that used by motorcycle racers. They should also wear full-face motorcycle helmets (right) to protect their heads and faces, the racers' most vulnerable parts.*

**THAT'S THE WAY TO DO IT!**
The best and most successful downhill racers rely on a combination of riding skills and physical strength. ...shing and to help them accelerate all the way down the ...ill racers try to keep their bikes on the ground, rather ...g jumps for the crowd. It's the fastest way!

A specialized do
is totally unlike
suspension syste
suspension syste
brakes help the

To avoid cra
course, downl
than performi

# All The Way!

Mountain bike events are designed to be fun and challenging. Competitors need to be fit and prepared to take a few knocks along the way! They also need to be able to carry out their own technical repairs — no assistance can be given during a race.

*Serious faces show that it's time for the event to start (above).*

*Younger riders (left) enjoy the thrill of the competition and the fun of riding with others.*

## TRAINING

Serious riders need to train hard in order to race to the finish (*right*). They will often work with the help of a professional coach to bring them to the peak of their physical fitness.

*The only time that a competitor can accept assistance during an event is if he or she wants to be given some refreshment during the course (below) to replace lost energy and fluids.*

*Winning a race (right) means that you have everything right and that you are the best rider on the day. It's an effort that covers bike preparation, training, eating for maximum energy, and practicing good riding techniques. Well done!*

volvic Natural Mineral Water from France

mbr MOUNTAIN BIKE RIDER FINISH

# Keeping fit AND HEALTHY

Anyone can enjoy mountain biking as long as he or she is reasonably fit and healthy. You can improve your fitness by eating balanced meals of carbohydrates (*below*) (found in bread, potatoes, pasta, and rice), protein (found in meat, fish, eggs, milk, and cheese), and vitamins (found in fresh fruit and vegetables). If you are planning a ride more than an hour long, take some healthy snacks and water or fruit juice (*above*).

## GIMME A BREAK!

*If you go for a long ride, take along something to drink and some healthy snacks to give you energy. Mountain biking is fun — but it can be hard work!*

## WARMING UP

It is a good idea to warm up your muscles with a few gentle stretches (*below*) before you set off on a long ride. Stretching before and after physical activity will help to prevent your muscles from stiffening up. Your legs do a lot of work when you ride your bike. In your warm-up and cool-down (after your ride) include a stretch for your calf muscles 1 , a stretch for the front of your thighs 2 and a stretch for the back of your legs 3 .

## FULL OF ENERGY

Whenever you are involved in a physical activity, such as mountain bike riding, your body loses energy. To replace this, you need to eat healthy snacks. Avoid fatty foods or foods and drinks that have lots of added sugars. These only give you a temporary burst of energy. Choose "energy bars" or snacks such as bananas or dried fruits.

1

2

3

## TIM GOULD

Tim Gould (*below*) is one of the world's best mountain bikers. His specialty is hill-climbing, an event in which he has won most of the hill-climbing competitions at mountain bike races around the world. Tim Gould is also an excellent cross-country racer. Helped by his hill-climbing skills, he is better in mountainous cross-country races than in those on flatter terrain.

## IT'S ALL DOWNHILL!

Before you attempt to go down a steep hill you must understand how your brakes work and how to use them (*see page 15*). Just before you approach the hill, shift into a high gear (*see pages 14-15*) to give you control over your pedals. Keep your weight toward the back of the bike to keep the bike from toppling over forward. With your weight at the back, the front wheel is free to track over lumps and bumps. Control your speed by pumping on the rear brake. Avoid pulling on the front brake too hard, otherwise you will stop the front wheel and go hurtling over the top.

*Some riders lower the seat (see page 13) in order to keep the correct position for downhill riding, with the weight toward the rear of the bike (left).*

# Regular TECHNIQUES

From tackling steep hills to avoiding obstacles in your path, off-road mountain biking is full of variety! You need the techniques to meet the challenges of the terrain over which you are riding. As with any new activity, it takes patience and practice (*right*) to perfect the skill of good mountain bike riding. The more you ride, the easier it will become. Pick up some tips by watching more experienced riders.

### BETTER BRAKING
*To stop your bike more quickly, use the front brake more often. Don't pull too hard or you will fly over the handlebars. Practice stopping, using only the front brake on a flat surface. Keep the braking power even so that the wheel doesn't "lock" and slide, or throw you off the bike. Don't try this going downhill at high speed.*

### FIRST STOP!
*Stay safe by learning to stop quickly* (above and right) *before you learn to ride fast.*

### IT'S ALL UPHILL!
Going up a steep hill (*right*) is a balancing act that needs lots of practice. Keep your weight over the front wheel but not so far forward that you lose any road grip, or traction, on the rear tire. Shift to a low gear (*see pages 14-15*) before the hill becomes really steep! Crouch down to bring your upper body nearer to the handlebars than when riding on flat terrain. Soon, you'll be riding up slopes that some people would have difficulty walking up!

# Advanced TECHNIQUES

The more you ride, the more you can improve your basic techniques so that your ride is faster, more comfortable, and more controlled.

For advanced moves, such as the bunny-hop, develop the ability to transfer your weight on your bike skilfully and smoothly. Move your weight backward to reduce the weight on the front wheel. Move your weight forward to lighten the weight on the rear wheel. To alter the amount the bike leans when you take a corner, transfer your weight from side to side.

Soon you will be able to make the bike do anything you want!

## JUMPS
Hitting a small bump in the trail can lift the bike into the air. Jumping is great, but because the bike is in the air, you're in more danger of hurting yourself. Start with small jumps; only progress to larger ones when you are confident. When you land, bend your arms and legs to reduce the impact of the bike as it lands.

## CORNERING AT SPEED
To corner at speed, as shown in the sequence (*right*), keep the leg and pedal on the outside of the turn in a downward position. Keep the leg on the inside of the turn away from the pedal, ready to put it down in case you lean too far over.

Professional riders "drift," or skid, through corners, steering in the opposite direction to control a skid with both wheels sliding sideways, and applying the brakes. It's dramatic — but best left to the professionals!

## THE BUNNY-HOP

*The bunny-hop allows you to lift both wheels off the ground. To look at it you'd think it was impossible but it's not! It is a useful move, especially if you come across a log or a pothole on the trail.*

*Begin with a single wheel bunny-hop. Ride at a walking pace, crouch down, and pull back on the handlebars as you push down on the pedals.*

*As you do this the front wheel will lift off the ground. Shift your weight forward, pushing down on the handlebars. This will lift the back wheel off the ground as the front wheel clears the obstacle. As you land, start to pedal.*

*For the double-wheel bunny-hop (above sequence), stay out of the seat and crouch down. Pull on the handlebars and jump, or spring, the bike clear of the obstacle. Not easy, but practice makes perfect.*

## ALL PUMPED OUT

Mountain bike riding is hard work — for your tires! At some point it is quite likely that your bike will suffer from a flat tire (below). Be prepared! Always carry a pump, a spare inner tube, a small set of tools, and a flat tire repair kit when you go for rides. Being able to mend a flat tire on the trail will save you from having to push your bike home, which is not much fun. Many flat tire repair kits come with easy-to-follow instructions.

## IN THE WORKSHOP

It's useful to have a place such as a corner of a garage or spare room to mend (below), clean, maintain, and adjust your mountain bike (left). Ask your parents or caregiver if you can use the room! Cover the floor with cardboard to keep any oil or mud from damaging the carpet. Store your tools neatly, cleaning them after use. Get a tool box to keep your tools in, and try to buy things, such as brake blocks and oil, before you need them.

Turn your bike upside down; spin the wheel to check that it is "true" — not wobbly.

Check that the quick-release lever for the rear wheel is not loose.

## ALL OILED UP

Bicycle chain oil is designed to make the chain run quietly and to stop it wearing out quickly (right). It's best to use a mountain bike oil. Keep it away from your brakes — even if they squeak!

## TOOLS FOR THE JOB

Your bike doesn't require a huge workshop to keep it running. All you need to give your bike a long and healthy life is a selection of wrenches, Allen wrenches, a screwdriver, and a can of oil — and a small book on bike maintenance.

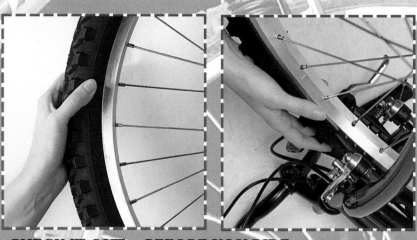

*CHECK IT OUT... BEFORE YOU RIDE*
Before you ride your bike, check these points:
❁ Are the tires inflated properly (*above left*)?
❁ Do the brakes work?
❁ Are the wheels fixed tightly into the frame?

❁ Are the gears working?
❁ Are the handlebars secured firmly?
❁ Is the seat at the correct height?

*CHECK IT OUT... REGULARLY*
Every month, check these points:
❁ Are the chain and the gear cables well-oiled? This will keep the bike running smoothly.
❁ Have the brake pads worn away? If so, make sure you replace them.

❁ *SAFETY FIRST* ❁
Don't work on your bike, especially your brakes, without having a responsible adult to check them for you afterward. Loose or badly adjusted parts could cause an accident.

*Hold the front wheel between your legs. Rock the handlebars from side to side to check they are not loose.*

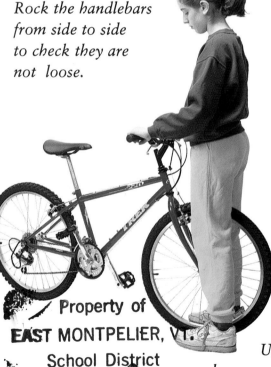

Property of
**EAST MONTPELIER, VT.**
School District

# Care and
# REPAIR

A regular care and repair check will keep your bike in good working order. Some parts of your bike, such as the brake blocks, wear out with use. It is essential for your safety that you check your bike (*see above*) and adjust and replace parts as necessary. If you follow a manual (ask your bike store to recommend one), you will be able to keep your bike safely on the road for as long as possible.

**ALL CLEANED UP**
*Mountain bikes get muddy or dusty when ridden off-road. Use water and a soft brush to clean your bike, and use a toothbrush to clean the hard-to-reach areas. Rinse the bike with clean water, either from a watering can or a hose (right). Oil the chain to prevent it from rusting.*

*Carry lights, a set of bike tools, and a flat tire repair kit (left) with you.*

# Upgrading your MOUNTAIN BIKE

When parts of your bike wear out, you can replace them with better parts. By upgrading your bike, you can improve its performance. You will also be able to build a better bike from the one you already have, without having to start from scratch.

With a good set of tools, you can upgrade your bike yourself, asking an adult to check it before you ride. Or, for a fee, your local mountain bike store will be able to upgrade your bike.

*Special cycling shoes have a mechanism that clips into these "clipless" pedals (left).*

**BRAKES**
*These "V" brakes (right and below left) are more powerful than other brakes fitted to a standard mountain bike. They are reasonably priced and a good addition to any bike, although you will probably need new brake levers, too.*

**WHY UPGRADE?**
Replacing parts such as tires, pedals, or gears as they wear out lets you improve the specification of your bike, fine-tuning your bike for your needs.

For instance, you can choose tires that will be most suitable for the type of terrain over which you ride. If you ride mostly on roads, then you can upgrade your bike with a smooth tire that has a smaller diameter. If you ride mostly over muddy ground, you will be better off upgrading your bike with a tire that has a rougher tread pattern, as shown in the bike below.

**SUSPENSION FORKS**
*To give you a more comfortable ride over rocky terrain, suspension forks can be added to your bike. Made from aluminum, with rubber springs inside, they compress, or squash down 3 inches to take the bumps out of the trail.*

# Tricks and STUNTS

When you are experienced at riding your bike you can try some tricks and stunts.

Only attempt a trick or stunt that you are sure is within your ability. There is no point in doing a trick or stunt that is too difficult and may result in a serious injury. Always wear a helmet and practice in a clear, safe path or area, well away from traffic, pedestrians, and horse riders.

## THE ENDO

An endo (*see sequence right and main picture*) is one of the few moves on a mountain bike in which the rider deliberately tips him or herself forward to balance over the front wheel.

An endo is a controlled stop where the bike rocks forward on the front wheel, then back onto both wheels. From a regular riding position 1, the rider moves his or her body weight toward the handlebars so that the rear wheel begins to lift 2. The rider lifts the rear wheel higher still by pushing down on the pedals while pulling his or her weight over the rear wheel 3. As the rear wheel lowers to the ground, the rider smoothly returns to a regular riding position 4.

Don't try this at high speeds — walking speed is fine — anything faster is dangerous.

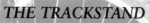

## THE TRACKSTAND
The trackstand (*left*) is tricky but fun. Use balance skills to stay on a stationary bike — with no feet on the ground! It helps if you point the front wheel up a gentle hill. You can then pedal and freewheel slightly, rocking the bike to keep your balance.

## THE WHEELIE

*By pedaling hard in a medium gear (see pages 14-15), while pulling back on the handlebars, it's possible to lift the front wheel off the ground, as in the first step for the bunny-hop (see pages 26-27). If you can do this and keep pedaling — then you're doing a wheelie! As well as good balance skills (see page 27), a good wheelie (above) depends on the rider being able to transfer his or her weight smoothly while pedaling evenly.*

### THE SWITZERLAND SQUEAKER

No one is sure why this trick is called the Switzerland Squeaker, but it is definitely one of the most difficult tricks around. The rider does an endo (*see page 34*), then moves his or her feet onto the front tire (*above*). He or she then pedals the bike backward by moving his or her feet on the front wheel. Really good riders do this trick without a rear wheel (*left*) — even harder! This is definitely not one to try at home — but it is good to know how the professionals do it!

❋ The rider removes his or her rear wheel.

❋ He or she applies the front brake.

❋ The rider places his or her feet on the front tire.

❋ The bike rolls backward as the rider uses the front brake for balance.

### ❋ NEVER ATTEMPT ANY OF THESE STUNTS.

*HANS RAY*
This German-born American rider (*right*) was the first person to develop mountain bike trick riding. Hans Ray began riding on small BMX-wheeled bikes before he began trying out an amazing range of tricks and stunts on mountain bikes. Today, Hans Ray rides professionally for a mountain bike team called Team GT. As well as competing and giving demonstrations around the world, Hans Ray helps to develop and improve the design of strong mountain bikes.

# Professional tricks
## AND STUNTS

These are some of the tricks that only professional stunt-riding mountain bikers can do. NEVER attempt to do these tricks yourself — leave them to the professionals. Many of these tricks developed from BMX display routines but are now performed by mountain bikers on their larger bikes.

Top stunt riders specialize in certain skills, such as distance wheelie or bunny-hopping competitions in which the rider repeats the trick many times along a course.

**THESE STUNTS ARE FOR PROFESSIONAL RIDERS ONLY. NEVER ATTEMPT THEM YOURSELF.**

*From a standard wheelie (see page 35), a stunt rider moves smoothly into a no-hander wheelie (above and right).*

*LOOK — NO HANDS!*
*If you think a normal wheelie is difficult, imagine trying to do a wheelie without using your hands!*

*Top riders can wheelie with one hand, and some with no hands at all, by balancing the bike simply with the weight of their bodies.*

*This isn't the sort of trick that's useful for riding a bike but it is fun to watch. Remember though — don't try it yourself. Stunt riders have trained for years so they can perform these tricks safely.*

# Have fun
## STAY SAFE!

Your mountain bike is a great way to keep fit, to have fun, and to see the countryside — but you must always be aware of safety. Have a pre-ride check and regularly maintain your bike (*see pages 30-31*). Only attempt moves for which you have the right skills and always follow the on- and off-road rules (*see page 15 and below right*). Take a basic first aid kit (*top right*) with you on long rides. You can seriously injure yourself, or someone else, if you take unnecessary risks. Remember, enjoy yourself... and be careful out there.

*FIRST AID*
*Don't move a person who has had a bad crash. He or she may have a back or neck injury that can result in paralysis if the person is moved. Leave someone with them and send someone for help.*

*As well as your lights, helmet, and some refreshments, you will need to take along with you a sense of humor! You may well get very muddy (below) and wet — enjoy it!*

**BE SEEN**
If you think you may be out on your bike when it gets dark, take your lights (*left*). Check before you leave that the lights are working. It is a good idea to take with you a set of spare batteries. Wear a bright reflective strip to help other road users see you — on- and off-road.

*MOUNTAIN BIKING RULES*
* Always wear a helmet.
* Respect other road and trail users.
* Make sure your bike is well-maintained and safe.
* Only ride where you can legally do so.
* Don't "trick ride" on roads.
* Carry tools, a flat tire kit, and a first aid kit with you.
* Always tell your parents or caregiver where you are going.
* Try to travel in a group.
* BE CAREFUL AND HAVE FUN!

# Mountain Bike Words

**BMX** A bicycle with small wheels designed for stunts, tricks, and racing.

**Brakes** The movement of the brake lever pushes the brake pad onto the rim, slowing down and stopping the bike.

**Bunny-hop** A trick that involves "jumping" the bike off the ground.

**Cable** A length of wire that controls the gears and brakes.

**Chainrings** The cogs at the front of the bike that give different gear ratios.

**Chain set** A term used for the cranks and chainrings.

**Clipless pedals** Pedals without toe clips but to which special bike shoes can be attached.

**Cogs** Small "teeth" at the front and rear of the bike that are driven by the movement of the gears and the chain.

**Crank** The arm that attaches the pedal to the chain.

**Cross-country racing** A race that goes over a variety of tracks and terrains.

**Downhill racing** A race that goes downhill only.

**Dual slalom** A downhill race in which riders compete in twos.

**Endo** A trick in which the rider tips forward over the front wheel without falling off.

**Frame** The collection of tubes that are welded together to form the main part of the bike.

**Freewheeling** Riding without pedaling.

**Gears** The chain moves from gear to gear across the chainrings and sprockets. In a low gear, the wheel spins more slowly to every turn of the pedal. In a high gear, the wheel spins faster to every turn of the pedal.

**Grips** The rubber covers that are fitted onto the handlebars.

**Headset** Contained within the head tube, the bearing in which the fork tube rotates.

**Hub** The part of the bike that contains the axle and bearings.

**Indexing** A system of gears in which the gears click from position to position.

**Off-road** Any riding that is not on a road.

**Rim** The part of the wheel that the tire sits on.

**Shifters** The levers on the handlebars that allow you to change gear.

**Sprockets** The cogs at the rear of the bike, driven or turned by the movement of the chain.

**Suspension** The part of the bike that is supported by a spring that moves when it is hit by a bump.

**Terrain** The ground over which you ride.

**Toe clips** Attachments on the pedal, used with a toe strap, to help secure the foot to the pedal.

**Traction** The grip that the tire has on the road.

**Trail** An off-road track over which you ride.

**Trail riding** Riding distances over hills or off-road.

**Tread** The pattern on the tire that helps to grip the road.

**Trials** A competitive event in which riders perform stunts.

**Upgrades** New and improved parts to add to a bike.

**Wheelie** A trick in which you ride with the front wheel off the ground.

# Index

Photo Credits: *Abbreviations: t-top, m-middle, b-bottom, r-right, l-left*

All the pictures in this book are by Steven Behr of Stockfile apart from the following
pages: back cover – Frank Spooner Pictures; 4-5, 8-9, 10 all, 11l & inset, 12t & b, 13t
& r, 14b, 25tl, 25ml all, 25b all, 30-31m, 31t inset, 31bl, 32-33, 33tl, 33m & 38t –
Roger Vlitos; 6tr & 26m – Bob Allen/Stockfile; 18tl – Seb Rogers/Stockfile.

The publishers would like to thank Trek UK, The Yellow Jersey, London, and Steve and
Jill Behr of Stockfile for their help and cooperation in the preparation of this book.